MAMMALS

David Burnie

KINGFISHER
NEW YORK

KINGFISHER

LONDON & NEW YORK

Copyright © Kingfisher 2011
This edition published 2014 by Kingfisher

Published in the United States by Kingfisher,
175 Fifth Ave., New York, NY 10010
Kingfisher is an imprint of Macmillan Children's Books, London.
All rights reserved.

Distributed in the U.S. by Macmillan,
175 Fifth Ave., New York, NY 10010

Illustrations by: Peter Bull Art Studio, Barry Croucher,
Gary Hanna (www.the-art-agency.co.uk)

Library of Congress Cataloging-in-Publication data has been applied for.

ISBN: 978-0-7534-7130-2

Kingfisher books are available for special promotions and premiums.
For details contact: Special Markets Department, Macmillan,
175 Fifth Ave., New York, NY 10010.

For more information, please visit www.kingfisherbooks.com

Printed in China
1 3 5 7 9 8 6 4 2
1TR/1113/WKT/UG/128MA

Note to readers: The website addresses listed in this book are correct at the time of publishing.
However, due to the ever-changing nature of the Internet, website addresses and content can change.
Websites can contain links that are unsuitable for children. The publisher cannot be held responsible for
changes in website addresses or content or for information obtained through third-party websites.
We strongly advise that Internet searches should be supervised by an adult.

CONTENTS

WORLD OF MAMMALS

The first mammals lived side by side with the dinosaurs, more than 200 million years ago. Dinosaurs died out, but mammals survived to become the most successful animals on Earth. They vary hugely in size and live on land, in water, and even in the air. But all mammals share three special features—they are warm-blooded, they have hair or fur, and they raise their young on milk.

Staying warm

Most mammals are covered with fur, which helps keep their bodies warm. Swimming mammals often have fat instead, just under their skin. A walrus's fat can be 6 in. (15cm) thick. It uses its bushy "mustache" to find food on the seabed.

Unlike small bats, fruit bats are vegetarians, tracking down fruit by its color and smell.

Together with okapi, giraffes make up a small family of African mammals. They have long necks and tongues.

The elephant family includes three species—two from Africa and one from Asia.

Anteaters have long snouts without any teeth. They live on the ground or in trees.

 The world's lightest mammal is the Etruscan shrew. It weighs only about 0.7 oz. (2g).

We are family

Scientists divide mammals into about 150 different families. The mammals in some families, called marsupials, raise their young in a pouch. Others, called placentals, raise their young inside the mother's body. Placental mammals include humans, and also blue whales—the biggest animals that have ever lived.

⊖ NEW DISCOVERIES

So far, scientists have identified about 5,500 kinds of mammals, but new animals are still being discovered every year. They include the Annamite striped rabbit, with distinctively patterned fur, from the forests of Southeast Asia. It was first seen by scientists in 1999. It feeds at night, but little else is known about how it lives.

Annamite striped rabbit caught on camera

Orcas, or killer whales, have pointed teeth and hunt large prey.

Zebras belong to a large family of plant-eating mammals with a hard hoof on each foot.

Most lemurs live in trees, but the ring-tailed lemur spends a lot of its life on the ground.

The gray kangaroo is one of the largest marsupials. It can bound at speeds of up to 30 mph (50km/h).

Brown rats are rodents—mammals with gnawing teeth.

Tigers belong to the cat family. Like most cats, they hunt on their own and feed entirely on meat.

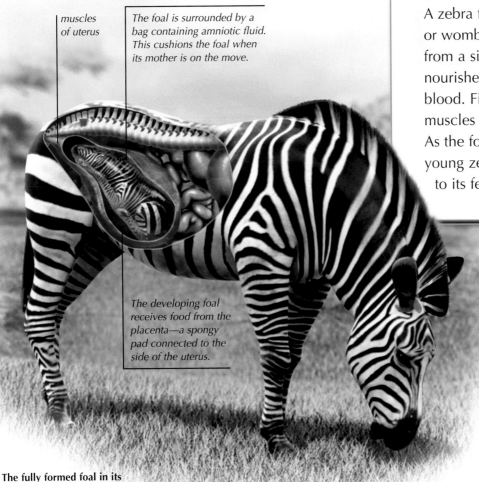

muscles of uterus

The foal is surrounded by a bag containing amniotic fluid. This cushions the foal when its mother is on the move.

The developing foal receives food from the placenta—a spongy pad connected to the side of the uterus.

The fully formed foal in its mother's uterus, shortly before being born.

Into the outside world

A zebra foal develops inside its mother's uterus, or womb, over one year. During this time, it turns from a single cell into a complete, new animal, nourished by substances circulating in its mother's blood. Finally, the big day comes. Powerful muscles push the foal out of the mother's body. As the foal takes its first breaths, its mother licks the young zebra dry. Within minutes, the foal totters to its feet and starts to feed on its mother's milk.

Unlike a human baby, the newly born foal emerges feet-first.

STARTING LIFE

Few moments are as dramatic as a zebra's birth, when a young foal emerges onto Africa's grassy plains. Like most mammals, zebras develop inside their mothers, so they are already partly grown at birth. Other mammals start life in a different way. Marsupials are born hairless and blind and develop in a pouch, while platypuses and echidnas hatch from tiny eggs. Despite these differences, all mammals start life on the same nutritious food: their mother's milk.

Egg-laying mammals
Platypuses and echidnas are the only mammals that lay eggs. This young echidna—or puggle—has hatched inside its mother's pouch and will stay safely inside it for at least six weeks.

 > Many mammals give birth to a single young, but some rodents have as many as 25 offspring.

Free ride

Some young mammals cling to their mother, using their claws to hold onto her fur. Female sloths hang upside down, so their babies can lie on them like a hammock.

Sloths usually have a single young, so there is plenty of room for it to travel on board its mother.

Zebras usually lie down to give birth, but many other mammals give birth standing up.

⊖ EARLY BIRTH

Newborn kangaroos look like small, pink grubs. At first, only their front legs work. They use them to pull their way through their mother's fur and into her pouch. There, the baby kangaroo, or joey, locks onto one of the mother's teats and starts to feed. Up to six months later, the joey finally moves out. Often, the next joey is already inside.

newly born joey

gray kangaroo with four-month-old joey

The newly born foal takes its first drink of milk.

A foal is born with an instinct to suck milk from its mother's teats, or nipples.

CARNIVORES—*a group of meat-eating mammals that includes cats, wolves, bears, and their relatives*

A BETTER BITE

"If you can't bite, don't show your teeth."

Old Yiddish proverb

Reacting to danger, the mountain lion, or puma, reveals its fearsome teeth. Its backward-pointing ears are another warning sign, telling other animals not to come close.

Many animals have teeth, but only mammals have teeth that are differently shaped. Together, a mammal's teeth work like a toolkit, letting it deal with its food. Plant-eating mammals have teeth for biting and for chewing, while predatory kinds have teeth that can grip, slice, crush, or even crack open bones. Predators sometimes use their teeth to drag away food—a grizzly bear's teeth are strong enough to move a horse.

Toothless mammals

Adult anteaters do not have any teeth. They do not need them, because they collect insects using their amazingly long tongue and then swallow them whole. Their stomach grinds up their food, helped by the grit that they eat.

◉ TOOLS OF THE TRADE

Scientists often identify mammals from their skulls and teeth. A hyena's teeth crack open bones, while a dolphin's teeth are shaped for catching fish. The crab-eating seal has strangely round-lobed teeth. Despite its name, the seal feeds on tiny animals, using its teeth like a sieve.

Crab-eater seals have teeth with rounded lobes like stubby fingers.

Dolphins have dozens of long, pointed teeth.

Hyena teeth can shatter bones, which the hyena swallows and digests.

 > Dolphins are the toothiest mammals. They have a single set of up to 252 teeth.

Muscles closing the jaws reach as far as the top of the head.

Grip and slice

The mountain lion—also known as a cougar or puma—belongs to a group of mammals called carnivores, which feed on meat. They have long canines, or eye teeth, which are the right shape for stabbing and gripping their prey. Behind them, bladelike teeth called carnassials slice through freshly killed flesh. Like most mammals, mountain lions have two sets of teeth. Their milk teeth have short roots and are replaced by bigger, permanent teeth as the animals grow into adults.

www.amnh.org/ology/features/stufftodo_zoology/superteeth.php

The carnassials (red) are near the back of the mouth, where the bite is stronger. Canine teeth (yellow) are on either side of the incisors at the front of the mouth.

WEANING—the change from the mother's milk to a more grown-up diet

Sharp vision picks up the slightest sign of movement against the snow.

Ears swivel back and forth to pick up sounds—a feature shared by dogs, which are descended from wolves.

HUNTING IN A PACK

Instead of hunting alone, gray wolves often live and hunt in packs. It is an efficient way of life because it lets wolves prey on animals that are too big and too strong for them to tackle on their own. A pack usually contains up to 12 adult wolves, led by a dominant— or "alpha"—pair. The dominant pair mate for life and produce all the pack's young. When they are too old to breed, younger members of the pack take their place.

Closing in

After a long chase through Canada's wintry landscape, a pack of wolves closes in on a moose. Moose are the world's largest deer—a big adult male can weigh more than 1,100 lb. (500kg), which is more than ten times as much as an average arctic wolf. But numbers and stamina count. Guided by their sharp senses, the wolves move in to make the kill.

 Despite their bad reputation, wolves have hardly ever been known to attack people.

Call of the wild

Wolf packs stake out a territory so that they have enough space to hunt. They claim territory by marking it with scent and by howling. Their eerie chorus keeps neighboring packs away.

Despite its powerful body, the moose is not a good fighter. Its antlers are for show rather than for attack.

Something for everyone

After most hunts, all the wolves usually eat some part of the kill. Meat is carried back to the den for cubs that are being weaned. In good times, wolves bury half-eaten food, consuming it weeks or even months later.

⊖ SNAP ATTACK

wolves surround the moose

moose's hindquarters vulnerable to attack

moose forced to stand its ground

The end of the hunt comes when the wolves surround the moose, cutting off its escape route. With the moose in snapping range, they dart forward to bite its unprotected underside or grip its muzzle tightly in their jaws. The moose spins around to fend off the attacks but finally falls as the pack moves in.

SELF-DEFENSE

At the first sign of trouble, most mammals try to make an emergency escape. Some run, while others swim or fly, but a small number (mostly plant eaters) use special defenses to stand their ground. They include pangolins, which have built-in armor plating, as well as porcupines, which are protected by hundreds of hollow quills that are long, stiff, and very sharp. When fully raised, they can keep an adult lion at bay.

An African porcupine's quills have backward-facing barbs that catch on skin and make them hard to pull out.

> An African porcupine's quills can be 12 in. (30cm) long. American porcupines have shorter and softer quills.

Two against one

With its back facing danger, an African porcupine tries to fend off two hungry lions. The lions are intent on flipping it over, so they can reach its furry underside. Each time they move closer, the porcupine rattles its quills and reverses. The quills can detach easily, embedding themselves in a lion's skin.

Chemical defenses

Performing a handstand, this skunk can squirt an awful-smelling fluid from glands beneath its tail. The fluid contains a high concentration of sulfur—the same substance that gives burning rubber its stomach-churning reek.

⊖ ARMOR PLATING

Millions of years ago, giant, armored mammals roamed Earth. Some were as big as cars. These giants eventually died out, but armored mammals still exist today, including armadillos, which are covered in bony plates, and pangolins, which have overlapping scales. Some kinds roll up to protect their soft body parts inside.

pangolin stops and tucks in its head when threatened

If quills get stuck in the skin, they remain embedded and can cause fatal wounds.

legs disappear beneath the pangolin's sharp-edged scales

Like most cats, lions can extend and retract their claws. This ensures that they are always sharp.

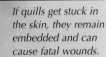

tail curls up, hiding the legs and head, and completing the ball

STRENGTH IN NUMBERS

In many parts of the world, rodents outnumber all other mammals put together. There are more than 2,000 kinds, living almost everywhere on land, as well as in rivers, streams, and ponds. Some are large, but most are small, fast-moving animals that try to stay out of sight. Rodents have sharp front teeth, and they gnaw through plants and seeds. Small rodents—such as mice and voles—breed at an amazing rate, but predators usually keep their numbers under control.

Productive parents
A female house mouse can have up to 80 babies per year. Blind and helpless at birth, her young grow up fast. By the age of ten weeks, they are fully mature and ready to have their own families.

golden-mantled ground squirrel

Cheeky
Like many small rodents, this North American ground squirrel has flexible cheek pouches, which work like shopping bags. It fills its pouches with seeds and then scampers to its burrow to store them underground.

Beavers gnaw through trees up to 10 in. (25cm) across, using their incisor teeth. These flat-bladed teeth have a self-sharpening front edge and long roots that curve toward the back of the jaws.

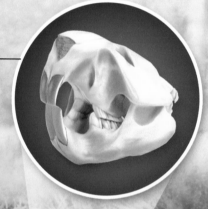

North American beaver dam

Beaver fur is waterproofed by a strongly scented natural oil, produced in glands near the tail.

⊖ GIANT RODENTS

Capybaras are the world's largest rodents. Looking like giant guinea pigs, they live in marshy places in South America, where they feed on waterside plants. Adult males measure up to 4.3 ft. (1.3m) long and can weigh as much as an adult man. Capybaras are related to guinea pigs, so the resemblance is not just skin-deep. But a capybara is specially adapted for swimming, with slightly webbed feet, and eyes and nostrils high up on its head.

Capybaras have barrel-shaped bodies and short legs.

> The largest-known beaver dam, in Canada, is 2,800 ft. (850m) long. It was found using satellite pictures in 2010.

"In time, a mouse will gnaw through a cable."

Dutch and German proverb

Skilled builders

Many animals build their own homes, but beavers are the only mammals that make dams across streams and rivers. It is a huge task, and they do it to protect their homes, or lodges, and to store winter food. To make a dam, beavers cut down waterside trees and skillfully float them into place. The dam is then sealed with mud and clay. Large dams are made by several generations of beavers and can be more than 50 years old.

The lodge is a hollow mound of branches, with concealed entrances below the waterline.

Small eyes, positioned high on the head, are covered by see-through membranes when diving.

Beavers chew through hard, old wood—as well as the soft saplings that they eat—using their powerful jaw muscles.

http://video.nationalgeographic.com/video/player/animals/beaver_lifecycle.html

FOLLOW THE LEADER

Hoofed mammals often spend their lives in herds. By staying together, they have a better chance of spotting danger and less chance of being singled out and attacked. Wildebeests and caribou form herds hundreds of thousands strong, but in the past, some antelope herds contained ten million animals and were more than 60 mi. (100km) long. Today, many farm animals live in herds, which makes them easy to control.

Wildebeests have curved, hollow horns. During the breeding season, males sometimes use them to ram their rivals.

Each front hoof has a gland that leaves a trail of scent. Wildebeests can use the scent to find their way back to the herd.

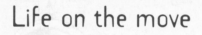

Life on the move

Surrounded by clouds of dust, common wildebeests migrate across Africa's Serengeti Plain. Every year, they travel up to 1,550 mi. (2,500km), allowing them to make the most of the seasonal rains. Wildebeests spend the dry season in wooded grassland, until instinct tells them that it is time to move. Gathering in huge lines, they stream across the landscape, giving birth to their calves on the way. By the time the wet season comes, the wildebeests arrive in lush grassland, where they feast on the annual burst of food.

> Most wildebeests give birth in a three-week "slot," so their young are almost exactly the same age as each other.

Time out

Wildebeests give birth out in the open, and their young soon follow the herd. Most deer and gazelles are different. This baby deer, or fawn, was born in thick undergrowth. It will stay hidden until it is several weeks old.

Swimming herds

In the Canadian Arctic, caribou spend the winters in forests and the summers in the open tundra. Their journey can be up to 3,100 mi. (5,000km) long—a record for a land mammal. On the way, they often have to swim across sea inlets and lakes.

Wildebeests travel together or in mixed herds with other mammals such as gazelles and zebras.

http://video.nationalgeographic.com/video/player/animals/wildebeest_migration.html

Defensive circle

Muskoxen live in the far north, where the biggest danger comes from wolves. If a herd is threatened, the adults form a defensive circle, with their massive horns facing outward and their young in the center.

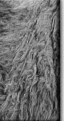

INSULATION—a body layer that helps stop an animal from becoming too warm or too cold

SURVIVING EXTREMES

Cells in the hump store fat—a substance that provides energy when food is hard to find.

Mammals live in some of the hottest, coldest, highest, and driest places on Earth. Unlike humans, they do not have special equipment or clothing, but they do have physical features that help them survive. These include amazingly warm fur, thick layers of body fat, and unusual body chemistry that lets them get all their water from their food.

Beating the heat

Like many small desert mammals, the long-eared jerboa digs burrows and avoids the daytime heat by feeding after dark. It eats seeds and insects and survives on "metabolic water"—water that it makes chemically from its food.

 range: deserts of Central Asia, from Mongolia to China

High life

Vicuñas live at altitudes of up to 1,800 ft. (5,500m), where the oxygen in the air is extremely thin. There, human hikers soon get tired, but vicuñas can run up steep slopes with ease. Their secret: special red blood cells that get the most oxygen from every breath.

range: Andes Mountains, from Peru to Chile

 > In the Arctic of northern Canada, some ground squirrels hibernate for nine months each year.

www.bbc.co.uk/nature/life/arctic_fox

Double protection

Bactrian camels live deep in Central Asia, where it is hot in the summer and freezing in the winter—and dry almost all the time. They store fat in their two humps, and they keep warm because of a long winter coat, which falls off in large patches during the spring.

range: deserts of Central Asia, from Mongolia to China

A camel's undercoat is made up of fine hairs that trap air, creating an insulating layer that keeps its body warm.

Winter wrap

The arctic fox is one of the world's most cold-proof mammals, thanks to its exceptionally thick winter fur. It can survive in temperatures as low as -58°F (-50°C), using its bushy tail to protect its feet and face from the icy wind. In the spring, its white winter coat is replaced by a much thinner one that is colored brownish-gray.

range: High Arctic, in North America, Europe, and Asia

⊖ HIBERNATION

Instead of battling through the winter, some mammals hibernate instead. They look like they are sleeping, but their bodies turn cold and their hearts beat only a few times per minute. Like machines on standby, they need only a small amount of energy to stay alive. Rodents often hibernate in burrows, while bats often choose caves or abandoned mines.

little brown bats hibernating

Party trick

Standing on its hind legs, a male African elephant reaches high up into a tree. Its trunk is a multipurpose tool. It can collect leaves, but the trunk can also lift huge weights or pick up scents in the air.

MODERN MAMMOTHS

Elephants are unique. No other mammals look like them or share their way of life. Weighing up to 7.7 tons (7 metric tons), they are the biggest land animals and the last survivors in a family that once included ice-age mammoths. Today, there are three species of these huge animals. In some places they are thriving, but in others they are threatened by illegal ivory hunters, as well as by a loss of forests and the spread of farms.

Huge cheek teeth grind up food. There are 24, but only four (two seen here on the top jaw) work at a time. Worn-out teeth move forward and then drop out.

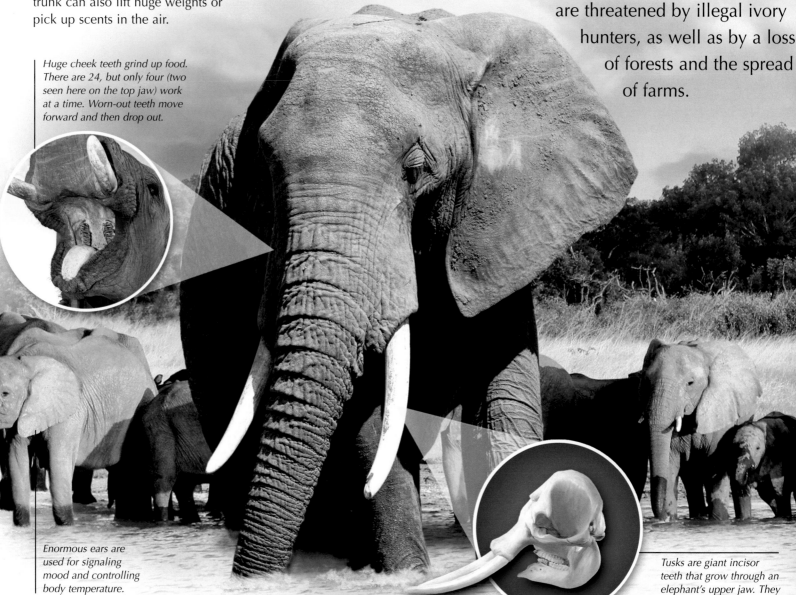

Enormous ears are used for signaling mood and controlling body temperature.

Tusks are giant incisor teeth that grow through an elephant's upper jaw. They are made mostly of ivory.

> The longest-known tusks from an African elephant measure just under 11.5 ft. (3.5m) from base to tip.

Leading by example

Elephant herds are based around females and their young. Each herd is led by a senior female, or matriarch, who leads the herd to food or water, following paths that she has memorized over many years. Female calves stay in the herd, but males leave it in their early teens. From then, they live in small groups, meeting females only when they mate. Female African elephants are ready to breed by the age of about ten. They have a single calf and feed it on milk for three or four years.

Elephants underground

In the mountains of Uganda, forest elephants march deep into caves to feed on salt. In their natural habitat, salty food is hard to find. Instead, they get this essential part of their diet by "mining" it underground.

Working elephants

African elephants are hard to tame, but Asian elephants have been kept in captivity for thousands of years. They are still used for ceremonial purposes, but now they are becoming rare in the wild.

This is an elephant carrying people dressed as historical figures in the Loy Krathong parade, in Thailand.

> "True philosophers are like elephants who, when walking, never place their second foot on the ground until the first is ready."
>
> **Bernard le Bovier de Fontenelle (1657–1757)**
> *French writer, from his book* Conversations on the Plurality of Worlds *(1686)*

The trunk can suck up water or dust without it getting into the elephant's lungs.

● TYPES OF ELEPHANTS

The savanna elephant and forest elephant both live in Africa. They have gigantic ears and trunks with two flexible tips. The Asian elephant is smaller and has a single tip on its trunk.

Asian   forest   savanna

www.bbc.co.uk/nature/life/african_elephant

SWIMMERS AND DIVERS

Most mammals can swim, even though they normally live on dry land. But some kinds are truly at home in the water and get all their food from the sea. Off the coast of California, sea lions and sea otters dive for food among forests of giant kelp, while elephant seals plunge far into the sea's depths to catch fish and squids. Seals and sea lions come ashore to breed, but the sea otter hardly ever sets foot on dry land.

Clash of the giants

Named after their inflatable trunks, male elephant seals can weigh up to 3.3 tons (3 metric tonnes). During the breeding season they fight for supremacy, rearing up and stabbing with their teeth. After walrus, elephant seals are the largest seals, or pinnipeds.

The fur is silky when young and short and sleek in adults.

Giant kelp is the world's biggest and fastest-growing seaweed. It forms large, offshore kelp forests.

A sea lion's front teeth include four long, pointed canines and two pointed incisors. Together, these six front teeth give a nonslip grip on the sea lion's prey.

sea lion hunting Pacific whiting— a favorite prey

Hunters in the kelp

Lean, agile, and intelligent, the California sea lion is a star performer in the wild and in captivity. It has long front teeth for gripping slippery fish. To swim, it uses its front flippers to propel forward and its hind ones to steer. On land, it bounds along on all four flippers, with its body off the ground. True seals, or phocids, are clumsier on the shore. They shuffle along on their stomachs, with their flippers by their sides.

> **PINNIPED**—*a carnivorous mammal with flippers and a streamlined body*

The front flippers have the same bones as a human arm and hand, although in different sizes. A web of leathery skin forms the flipper's blade.

Grazers in the sea

Most diving mammals are carnivorous, but dugongs and manatees eat underwater plants. They live in warm, shallow water and look like giant barrels drifting over the seabed. This dugong (above) is feeding on sea grass off the coast of Western Australia.

Offshore otter

The sea otter is the only otter species that lives almost entirely offshore. Diving down into the kelp, it uses its paws to collect small sea animals, deftly avoiding their pincers and spines. Instead of eating on the spot, it carries food to the surface, often tucking it into a fold of skin.

Sea otters stay warm by having the world's densest fur. The hairs trap a layer of air, keeping the skin dry and stopping the heat from getting out.

● LIFE AFLOAT

When sea otters are not diving, they spend a lot of time floating on their backs. It is a strange position for any mammal, but it has a lot of benefits. It lets females keep their young warm and dry. It also turns the otter's stomach into a floating worktop, where it cracks open shells by hitting them against a heavy stone.

sea otter nursing young

sea otter hunting crabs

❯ Elephant seals can dive up to 1 mi. (1.5km) deep and can stay underwater for more than an hour.

The sperm whale's large fluke drives it forward.

Measuring up to 89 ft. (27m) long, the blue whale is by far the world's biggest animal.

Family group

Whales, dolphins, and porpoise belong to a single family of mammals called the cetaceans. There are about 80 different kinds, from the mighty blue whale to the tiny vaquita, which is smaller than most seals. Cetaceans have nostrils, or blowholes, on top of their heads, which close up when they dive. Most cetaceans feed near the surface, but sperm whales and beaked whales dive to great depths to hunt.

WHALES AND DOLPHINS

Roaming the oceans, whales and dolphins spend their entire lives at sea. They include some of the greatest long-distance swimmers, as well as the largest animals. Not all are giants, but they share the same body plan, with streamlined bodies, two front flippers, and horizontal flukes, or tails. Most have teeth, but the largest whales are toothless. They filter small animals from the water, using mouths that work like giant sieves.

The sperm whale's huge head is filled with waxy oil, which adjusts its buoyancy during dives to feed on giant squids at up to 9,840 ft. (3,000m) deep.

A sperm whale's narrow lower jaw has up to 28 pairs of sharply pointed teeth. Each tooth is up to 8 in. (20cm) long—bigger than any other predator's.

 > There are nearly 20 kinds of beaked whales, but many of them have never been seen alive.

The blue whale's brushlike baleen plates trap small animals. The whale then swallows the food using its 2-ton tongue.

http://www.panda.org/what_we_do/endangered_species/cetaceans/about/blue_whale

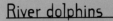

River dolphins

With slender jaws and tiny eyes, the Amazon river dolphin, or boto, looks different to sea dolphins. It uses echolocation to find its fish and turtle prey in muddy water. The only other continent where river dolphins are found is Asia.

Male narwhals have long, spiraled tusks, up to 10 ft. (3m) long. Males use them like horns in fights with rivals.

Orcas, or killer whales, are large dolphins with a tall fin on their backs. They live in groups, eating seals, sharks, and sometimes other whales.

Found worldwide, except near the poles, the bottle-nosed dolphin is fast, acrobatic, and intelligent. It lives in small groups, or pods, and eats fish and squids.

At just 5 ft. (1.5m), the vaquita is the smallest cetacean. This tiny porpoise lives only in a small area off Mexico and is critically endangered.

◉ ECHOLOCATION

Toothed cetaceans, such as dolphins and sperm whales, can use sound to find food. They make clicks that travel through the water and listen for echoes that bounce back from animals. This system, called echolocation, is also used by bats and a small number of other mammals, including shrews.

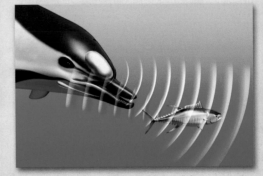

dolphin sound clicks hitting fish prey

Stranded

Each year, hundreds of whales, such as this pilot whale, are marooned on beaches, where they often die. Strandings happen because whales cannot sense the gradual slope where the seabed rises toward the shore.

Elastic grooves allow the throat to expand when the whale feeds. The whale filters out fish and krill using its baleen plates. It then tightens the grooves, so that its throat returns to its normal size.

"Strong against the tide, the enormous whale emerges as he goes."

Christopher Smart (1722–1777)
English poet, from his poem A Song to David *(1763)*

As the whale bursts upward, the front flippers make its body spin, while the final push comes from the horizontal fluke, or tail.

The whale's back arches as it rises into the air. Its body rotates and topples back toward the surface.

Whale tracking

Every humpback whale has unique tail markings. The whales often expose their flukes, so scientists use these markings to identify individual whales. This helps them track humpbacks when they migrate.

OCEAN GIANTS

Weighing up to 44 tons (40 metric tonnes), the humpback whale is one of the most extraordinary mammals in the seas. Everything about it is big—from its colossal appetite to its enormous flippers. Humpbacks are famous for their long migrations and for their amazingly complex underwater songs. They are natural acrobats, bursting upward through the surface in a maneuver called a breach, which ends in one of the biggest splashes in the animal world.

> Humpback songs can be more than 20 minutes long. They have musical "trends," which change slowly from year to year.

Breaching

Many whales breach, but few are as energetic as the humpback. During a breach, the humpback's body may almost entirely leave the water, before twisting and falling, so that it hits the surface on its side. Sometimes a whale breaches just once, but often it performs several breaches in a row for perhaps more than an hour. Scientists are not sure why whales breach. They may use it to attract partners or perhaps to clean parasites from their skin.

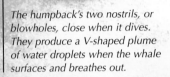

The humpback's two nostrils, or blowholes, close when it dives. They produce a V-shaped plume of water droplets when the whale surfaces and breathes out.

Each eye is about the size of a large orange and is protected from flowing seawater by a film of transparent oil.

The whale usually makes a half or quarter turn before it hits the surface, while breathing out in a powerful "blow."

Picked up an by underwater microphone, this humpback song may have traveled more than 120 mi. (200km) through the sea. Humpbacks probably use their songs in courtship and as a way of staying in touch.

⊖ BACK FROM THE BRINK

Until the 1960s, the humpback was widely hunted for its meat and its fat, or blubber. More than 90 percent of the world's humpbacks were killed. Today, humpbacks are protected by most nations and their numbers are recovering slowly. Even so, these whales risk colliding with large ships or getting caught up in fishing gear.

Whale watching has become a major attraction.

STAYING IN TOUCH

All mammals have to communicate, even if they spend most of their lives on their own. But for meerkats, staying in touch is a key part of daily life. Meerkats live in groups, or packs, and they use special calls to warn of danger as they search for food. Like most mammals, meerkats also leave signals in scent. These help mark territory around their burrows, warning other meerkats to stay away.

Martial eagles often weigh five times as much as meerkats and can carry them off in their claws.

An alarm signal for an eagle is a drawn-out call. When sounded, the entire meerkat pack vanishes underground.

The inner lining of the snout is full of nerves sensitive to smells and scent signals, or pheromones.

> Meerkats have emergency boltholes scattered across their territory, just in case they are attacked.

TREETOP CHORUS

At dawn and dusk, howler monkeys call across the treetops, producing some of the loudest sounds made by any animal on land. These leaf-eating monkeys live in small, slow-moving groups, and they use sound to stay in touch with neighbors. Males have a throat pouch that works like an amplifier, helping calls travel up to 3 mi. (5km.)

female (left) and male (right) howler monkeys calling

Intruder alert

Sentries watch out for danger, and they also sniff the air for meerkats from other groups, which have a "foreign" smell. Young male meerkats often move to new packs, searching for a chance to breed. Sometimes sentries let them in, but often the pack fights them off.

Adult cobras are dangerous enemies, especially if they get into the pack's burrows.

"As soon as there is life there is danger."

Ralph Waldo Emerson (1803–1882)
American writer and poet

Marker mounds

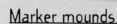

White rhinos leave their dung in communal mounds, called middens, giving the dung a kick to scatter it over the ground. By visiting a midden, a rhino can keep track of other rhinos in the area. It also leaves a signal to show when the rhino last passed by.

On the alert

Meerkats live in dry parts of southwest Africa, where they feed on insects and other small animals. They set off in a group, staying in touch with soft, twittering noises as they fan out over the ground. While most of the pack is busy feeding, sentries stand up on their back legs. They watch and listen, sounding the alarm if any predators or intruders head their way.

Scent signals

Rubbing a low branch with its face, this leopard is leaving a scent mark that will last for many days. The scent contains chemicals called pheromones, which work like a signaling system, allowing it to stay in touch with its own kind.

Propped up by their tails, sentries can keep watch for danger for up to an hour.

APES AND MONKEYS

With grasping hands and forward-facing eyes, apes and monkeys are great climbers, and many spend their lives in trees. Together with lemurs, bush babies, and tarsiers, they belong to a group of mammals called primates, which live mostly in warm parts of the world. Primates often have large brains for their size, and some are experts at solving problems and using tools. We are primates ourselves, and intelligence is one of the secrets of our success.

Like all lemurs, the indri is found only in Madagascar. It leaps from tree to tree with its body upright and its arms and legs thrown wide open.

Winter warmer

Japanese macaques live farther north than any other wild primate. They have extra-long fur to keep out the cold, and in the winter they lounge in hot springs to warm up. They are famous for their intelligence, learning new skills and passing them on.

Woolly spider monkeys, or muriquis, can feed hanging on by their tails. They live in Brazil's Atlantic forest— a threatened habitat that has almost disappeared.

The guereza is a leaf-eating monkey from Central and East Africa. It is white when it is born but gradually changes color to black and white.

Agile and intelligent, vervet monkeys are a common sight in East and southern Africa. They often come down to the ground and steal food in towns and on farmland.

> PREHENSILE—*describes a body part that is able to wrap tightly around something and hang on*

Primates of the world

There are about 250 types of primates. Most live in tropical forests, and although some are vegetarians, many eat a wide range of food, from leaves and fruit to insects and eggs. Primates have long arms and legs, with flexible fingers and toes, and many also have a prehensile tail that can hold all their weight. Eyes that face forward make primates good at judging distances. This is a vital skill when leaping from branch to branch.

Tarsiers, from Southeast Asia, are tiny primates that hunt insects at night. They watch for prey using their giant eyes and then leap on it through the dark.

● MAKING FACES

Over long distances, primates often stay in touch by sound, but when they get together, they communicate with their faces as well. This young chimp is making a "pout"—an expression that means that it is concerned or upset. In chimps, another common expression is the grin. Unlike a human grin, this often means that a chimp is afraid or eager to prevent a fight.

chimpanzee facial expression

Africa's gorillas are the world's largest primates, weighing up to 440 lb. (200kg). Despite their size and strength, they are harmless vegetarians, spending most of their time on the ground.

> The smallest primates are mouse lemurs from Madagascar—their bodies can be less than 4 in. (10cm) long.

FOREST LONERS

Orangutans look different to other apes, with their orange-red fur and amazingly long arms. They feed mostly on fruit and spend almost all of their lives in trees. Unlike chimpanzees and gorillas, they usually live alone, although youngsters stay with their mothers for eight years—one of the longest childhoods in the animal world. They are smart, quick to learn, and, despite their size, surprisingly agile.

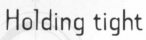

orangutan swinging through the trees

Young orangutans have light, delicate fur, but adults have coarse fur that is downward-trailing to help shed the rain. Orangutan fur color varies from orange to rusty red.

Holding tight

Orangutans are born with a strong grip, and they use it every minute of their lives. Baby orangutans cling to their mother's fur, while adults clamber along branches with their leathery hands and feet. Because orangutans are heavy, they can make slender trees sway under their weight. When a tree bends down, an orangutan steps off it and grabs one nearby—an efficient way of traveling above the forest floor.

Face flaps

Male orangutans can be twice as heavy as females and develop wide cheek flaps as they mature. They breed from the age of 15, but, unlike females, the males play no part in taking care of the young.

"Contrary to general belief, humans imitate apes more than the reverse."

Frans de Waal (born 1948)
Dutch primatologist

> There are two species of orangutans—one species lives in Sumatra, and the other lives in Borneo.

Nesting time

Orangutans spend the night in temporary nests, which they build high up in trees. During the day, they roam through the forest, collecting most of their food in the treetops and only occasionally coming down to the forest floor.

Orangutans eat more than 100 different types of fruit.

Unlike humans, orangutans have opposable big toes. This allows their feet to work like a second set of hands, clinging to branches or supporting their weight.

● USING TOOLS

In recent years, scientists have discovered that orangutans are at least as good as chimpanzees at making and using tools. They collect insects and honey with specially prepared sticks, and they have even been seen spear-fishing from forested riverbanks. They pass on new skills by watching and copying one another— something that is rare in the animal world.

GOING UNDERGROUND

COLONY—a group of animals from the same species that live together to improve their chances of survival

For small mammals, life in the open can be dangerous, because predators are never far away. To survive, many dig homes underground. There, they are safe from most of their enemies, although they still have to come to the surface to feed. But some mammals, including moles and mole rats, are fully subterranean. They get everything they need below ground and hardly ever see the light of day.

Touchy-feely

The star-nosed mole, from North America, finds small animals using a ring of 22 highly sensitive, fleshy tentacles that spread out around its nose. An excellent swimmer, the mole hunts in ponds and streams, as well as under the ground.

Loose-fitting skin helps mole rats to squeeze past each other. They huddle together for warmth since they have little body fat.

Mole rats eat large roots, or tubers. They often harvest food a little at a time, so that the plant keeps growing.

new tunnel leading to tuber

final member of the team kicks soil up onto the surface

Team spirit

Beneath the dry grasslands of East Africa, naked mole rats live in permanent groups, or colonies, containing workers ruled by a queen. These strange, bald rodents feed on the swollen roots of plants, using their incisor teeth to tunnel through the soil. A typical family contains up to 80 animals, but only the queen produces young. The workers take care of the queen and her offspring and dig burrows in head-to-tail teams.

active toilet area, or latrine

old latrine, sealed off from burrow system

The queen gives birth to up to 20 pups each time she breeds. She feeds them on milk until the workers take over, giving them solid food.

active latrine

 > European badgers inherit their burrows, or setts—some stay in use for more than 100 years.

Eyes and ears are small, but the face has highly sensitive whiskers. A mole rat also feels using hairs on its tail.

cluster of untouched tubers

Incisor teeth grow nonstop, making up for wear and tear. Cheeks seal off the mouth behind the incisors, so the mole rat does not swallow the soil.

lead member of the team bites off earth and kicks it backward

Attack from below

Bursting up through loose sand, a golden mole munches on a locust in Africa's Namib Desert. Some golden moles make permanent burrows, but those in deserts "swim" through sand. They find their prey by listening for faint sounds overhead.

◉ GIANT BURROWS

With powerful front claws, aardvarks dig record-breaking burrows, wide enough for a person to crawl inside. These piglike animals from Africa spend the day underground, emerging after dark to feed on termites and ants. Abandoned burrows are often used by other mammals, including warthogs, porcupines, and hyenas, and they are favorite areas for snakes.

aardvark emerging from burrow

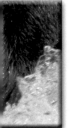

BEAR FACTS

With their massive bodies and powerful jaws, bears include the biggest predators on ice and on dry land. The polar bear weighs more than three quarters of a ton. The brown bear is just as large, with enough strength to kill and drag away a horse. Despite their size and strength, most bears are omnivorous, eating all kinds of food. Their menu ranges from fruit and seeds to fish, and even moths.

Bears have average eyesight, but their sense of smell is among the best of all mammals.

Brown bears have impressive incisors, but, unlike most carnivores, their rear teeth are shaped for crushing plant food, instead of for slicing up meat.

∨ OMNIVORE—an animal that eats all kinds of food, including meat and plants

Winter birth

Many bears give birth in the winter, which they spend tucked away inside dens. At first, the young are tiny, but they grow fast on their mother's milk. This female black bear has produced three cubs, which will leave her when they are 18 months old.

⊖ LEAFY LUNCH

The giant panda is the only bear that feeds almost entirely on plants. Every day, it eats up to a tenth of its weight in bamboo, sitting upright while it gathers and chews its food. Unlike other bears, each of its front paws has an extra, peglike "thumb" that it uses to hold bamboo stems.

panda eating bamboo

> There are eight kinds of bears—the smallest is the sun bear, from Southeast Asia.

Bear attack

Polar bears are some of the world's most dangerous mammals. They have an exceptionally good sense of smell and are quickly attracted by the scent of food. This one is trying to bite through a truck window, to get at the driver inside.

Paws are broad and flat, with strong claws for digging and climbing. Pads of skin give the paws a good grip, even on ice or slippery rocks.

Fatal jump

For North America's brown bears, the annual salmon run is an unmissable feast, as millions of fish swim upriver to lay their eggs. Brown bears wade into the fast-flowing rapids and try to catch the salmon as they leap through the air. Fish is a highly nutritious food, which is why salmon-eating brown bears are bigger than ones that live farther inland.

IN THE NIGHT SKY

When darkness falls, some of the strangest animals take to the air. Gliding mammals launch themselves from trees, while bats speed through the dark, homing in on insect prey. Most gliders travel short distances, buoyed by flaps of elastic skin. Bats have real wings, made of leathery skin. They can stay airborne for hours, and some travel hundreds of miles when they migrate.

To launch, the glider kicks itself off a tree.

flight membrane has thick edge

large eyes work well in dim light

To steer, the flat underside of the tail acts as a rudder.

To land, the glider's body is steeply angled.

Gliding membrane, or patagium, connects the front and back legs. When not in use, it tightens up along the glider's sides.

Controlled descent

With skin flaps spread wide, the Australian sugar glider moves quickly and silently among the trees. It can travel more than 160 ft. (50m) in a single jump, controlling its glide by angling its body and steering with its tail. The sugar glider is a marsupial, but this way of moving is also used by some other mammals, including some rodents and flying lemurs, or colugos.

> Flying lemurs, or colugos, can glide up to 490 ft. (150m)—farther than any other mammal.

Highly folded nose leaf emits pulses of ultrasound. Large ears detect echoes that bounce off obstacles and flying insects.

short arm bones close to body

flight membrane connecting tail and legs

The wing membrane is stretched by thin and unusually flexible finger bones, which flick as the wing beats. This helps the bat zigzag through the air.

thin layer of double-sided skin

Powered flight

Bats are the only mammals with wings, and the only ones that use their own muscle power to stay in the air. Predatory kinds, or microbats, are extremely agile fliers. They find their prey by echolocation—the same system used by dolphins and whales—and often use their wings and tail to scoop prey toward their mouths.

flying insect prey found through echolocation

Fishing in the dark
Swooping low over the water, a Mexican bulldog bat snatches up a fish. Fish-eating bats sense ripples on the surface of lakes and ponds and use them to home in on their prey.

● PRIVATE SHELTERS

During the day, most insect-eating bats hide away in tree holes or in caves. These white tent-making bats, from Central America, have another way of staying out of sight. They bite through the underside of a large leaf, so that its sides drop down. The bats then crowd together inside, staying warm and dry.

tent-making bats under a leaf

Ready for takeoff

Flying foxes look different to bats that hunt insects. As well as being big, they have doglike faces and big eyes, sturdy back legs, and a long, bony thumb on each wing. When they are resting, they often wrap their wings around their bodies like a coat. Females keep their young warm and safe by tucking them up inside.

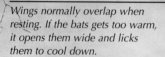

Wings normally overlap when resting. If the bats gets too warm, it opens them wide and licks them to cool down.

FLYING GIANTS

With wings up to 6 ft. (1.8m) across, flying foxes are bigger than most birds. Despite the name, they are not foxes but megabats— giant vegetarians that feed on fruit and flowers. Taking off as the sun sets, they speed over the treetops, using sight and smell to find food. Unlike most bats, flying foxes spend the day hanging from exposed branches high up in trees. These roosts, called camps, are full of activity, especially during the breeding season.

A mother bat wraps up her young in her wings.

> In Africa, some megabats migrate in "flocks" numbering hundreds of thousands of animals.

The wing membrane is light but tough, so that it does not tear when the bat lands in trees.

Flying foxes have a claw on their thumbs and on the second finger of each wing. They use their two thumb claws to walk upside down along branches and to get at food.

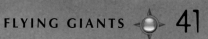

Messy eaters

Flying foxes are noisy and untidy feeders. They crash-land in trees and feed by lapping up pollen and nectar or by chewing fruit into a pulp. After swallowing the juice, they spit out the seeds, helping trees spread.

A flexible neck lets the bat look all around while hanging upside down.

DANGER ZONE

Despite their size, flying foxes have a lot of enemies. During the daytime, they are attacked by eagles and other birds of prey. After dark, they are ambushed by snakes and owls. With their giant wings, they also get tangled up in power lines and in nets that farmers use to protect their fruit crops.

carpet python at a flying fox camp

Whale wars

Since 1986, whales have been protected by a hunting ban, which forbids commercial whaling. Despite this, some hunting continues. In 2007, these inflatable whales in Sydney, Australia, were a protest against a decision by Japan to resume killing humpback whales.

MAMMALS IN DANGER

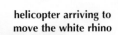

helicopter arriving to move the white rhino

Today, wild mammals face difficult problems. Many are threatened by disappearing forests, hunting, pollution, and climate change. The danger list includes some of the world's best-known creatures—such as tigers, rhinos, and giant pandas—as well as lots of smaller mammals that rarely make the headlines. Fortunately, the news is not all bad. Around the world, conservation projects are helping some critically threatened mammals survive.

The 3.3-ton (3-metric-tonne) rhino is heavily sedated, then rolled onto a net, which will be slung beneath the helicopter.

> The Javan rhino is one of the world's rarest mammals—only about 50 are left in the wild.

Airlift

With almost 18,000 animals in game parks and sanctuaries, the white rhino is off the danger list, but its survival depends on round-the-clock conservation. The main threat comes from poachers, who target white rhinos for their horns, one of which can be sold for thousands of dollars. As well as being protected, rhinos are actively managed to help their numbers grow. In South Africa, "spare" adults are flown by helicopter to new areas to expand the rhino's range.

Ear notching is a quick and relatively painless way of identifying a rhino. The notches are permanent and easy to see with binoculars.

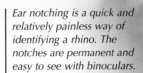

white rhino and calf

Primate crisis

In the next 50 years, more than half the world's primates, including orangutans, could die out in the wild. For most, the biggest threat is the destruction of their forest habitat, as people cut down trees for timber and to clear land for farming.

Back from the edge

Over the centuries, many horses escaped into the wild, but only Przewalski's horses from Mongolia are truly wild animals. They were saved from extinction in the 1900s through captive breeding. About 300 now live in the wild.

http://wwf.panda.org/what_we_do/endangered_species/rhinoceros

⊜ CAUGHT ON CAMERA

On the Asian island of Borneo, a rare Sundaland clouded leopard triggers off an automatic camera on the forest floor. This kind of equipment is making it easier to keep track of endangered species and to discover ones that are entirely new to science. This is especially true in forests and the deep ocean, where it is easy for animals to stay hidden.

Sundaland clouded leopard

GLOSSARY

altitude
Height above sea level. Most mammals live below 16,400 ft. (5,000m)—above this, few survive the cold or the thin air.

barb
A backward-pointing scale that makes something more difficult to dislodge.

breed
To have offspring. Before mammals can breed, parents have to pair up and mate.

buoyancy
A force that stops things from sinking. Most mammals are naturally buoyant, but some swimming mammals can reduce their buoyancy when they dive.

burrow
A home that is dug out underground. Many mammals dig their own burrows, using their feet or their teeth, but some take over burrows that have been abandoned by other animals.

canine
A pointed front tooth that mammalian carnivores use to grip their prey.

carnassial
A bladelike tooth that mammalian carnivores use to slice up meat.

carnivore
Any animal that eats meat. In mammals, the same word is also used for the family that includes cats, dogs, wolves, and their relatives.

cell
Cells are the microscopic units that make up all living things. A mammal's body contains more than 200 types of cells—each one has a different range of tasks.

colony
A group of animals, from the same species, that live together in an extended family.

courtship
Special forms of behavior that animals use during the breeding season, to help them attract a partner.

dominant
A high-ranking animal within a group. In lions, wolves, and many other mammals, only the dominant animals breed.

echolocation
Sensing food or the way ahead by making short bursts of sound and listening for echoes that come back.

fluke
The tail of a whale or a dolphin. Unlike a fish's tail, flukes are horizontal, and they do not contain any hard struts or bones.

glands
A small organ, in an animal's body or on its skin, that makes and releases special chemicals.

gnaw
To chew through food or obstacles using self-sharpening incisors, or front teeth.

herd
A group of mammals that stays together for most of their lives. Herds are usually made up of plant-eating mammals with hooves.

hibernation
A special kind of deep, winter sleep. It lets animals survive cold weather, using food stored inside their bodies.

hoof
A toe with a hard tip, made of the same substance found in fingernails. Hooves are found in large, plant-eating mammals, and they keep growing to make up for wear and tear.

ice age

A long period of intense cold, causing glaciers and icecaps to expand. The last ice age ended about 10,000 years ago.

incisor

Incisors are flat-edged front teeth that mammals use to nip and to gnaw.

instinct

Behavior that is built into a mammal's nervous system and so is not learned.

krill

Finger-size relatives of shrimp that live in huge swarms in polar seas. They make up an important source of food for whales and seals.

mammoth

A prehistoric member of the elephant family. Ice-age mammoths were often covered with long fur.

marsupial

A mammal that raises its young in a pouch. Most marsupials live in Australia and New Guinea, but some are found in the Americas.

membrane

A thin layer of living tissue, usually with its own blood supply and nerves.

migration

A long return journey between two parts of the world. Animals usually migrate with the seasons, so that they arrive at a good time to feed and breed.

nutritious

Full of nutrients—the substances that fuel an animal's body and let it grow.

omnivore

An animal that eats all kinds of food.

parasite

An animal that spends its life on or inside a much bigger animal, using it for food. Many parasites that attack mammals feed on their blood.

predator

An animal that hunts for its food.

prey

An animal that predators hunt for food.

rodent

A small- or medium-size mammal with front teeth that are specially shaped for gnawing.

species

A group of living things that look alike and that breed only with their own kind.

stamina

Endurance or staying power. Many predatory mammals use stamina to outrun their prey.

streamlined

Having a smooth outline that slips easily through water or through air. Streamlining is especially important for predators, such as sea lions, because they have to move fast to catch their prey.

subterranean

Anything that is underground.

territory

A piece of ground that an animal claims as its own, keeping rivals away. It usually contains enough food and space to raise a family.

tundra

The cold, treeless landscape found around the Arctic and near the tops of many mountains.

ultrasound

Pulses of sound that are too high-pitched for human ears to hear. Bats, dolphins, and other mammals use ultrasound to locate their food.

INDEX

INVESTIGATE

Find out about living mammals by visiting zoos and wildlife parks. Museums are also a great way to discover mammals from the past.

Wildlife parks and zoos

Modern zoos give mammals a lot of space and a habitat like their natural home. In wildlife parks, animals have more room to roam, letting them behave as if they were wild.

Ice-age mammoths had extra-long fur, protecting them against the bitter cold.

 Once a Zookeeper by Francis Lim (Carnegale)

 San Diego Zoo, San Diego, CA 92101

 www.sandiegozoo.org

A young chimp plays on a zoo climbing frame.

Museums and exhibitions

Most big natural history museums have displays showing how wild mammals live. Some also have fossils of prehistoric species, including giant kinds that lived during the last ice age.

 National Geographic Prehistoric Mammals by Alan Turner (National Geographic Children's Books)

 Smithsonian Museum of Natural History, Washington, D.C. 20560

www.mnh.si.edu

A cheetah watches for prey from a truck, during filming for a documentary.

Despite protection, tigers are still endangered and face an uncertain future in the wild.

Documentaries and movies

See some of the world's most spectacular mammals in close-up, thanks to documentaries and movies. If you have a camera, try taking your own photos of wild mammals in your area.

 *National Audubon Society Guide to Nature Psychology* by Tim Fitzharris (Firefly Books)

The Life of Mammals DVD (BBC Warner)

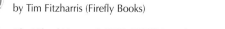 http://dsc.discovery.com/guides/animals/animals.html

Conservation groups

Many conservation organizations help protect mammals. Some are focused on individual species, while others aim to conserve all mammals in a country or region.

    Lions, Tigers and Bears: Why are Big Predators so Rare? by Ron Hirshi (Boyds Mills Press)

  The World Wildlife Fund, Washington, D.C. 20090

www.panthera.org/programs/tiger/save-tiger-fund

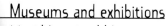